UNDEFEATED

UNDEFEATED

God's Strategy for Successful Living

Ambassador International
GREENVILLE, SOUTH CAROLINA & BELFAST, NORTHERN IRELAND

www.ambassador-international.com

Undefeated
God's Strategy for Successful Living

ISBN: 978-1-62020-533-4
eISBN: 978-1-62020-459-7

Cover Design & Typesetting by Hannah Nichols
Ebook Conversion by Anna Riebe Raats

AMBASSADOR INTERNATIONAL
Emerald House
427 Wade Hampton Blvd.
Greenville, SC 29609, USA
www.ambassador-international.com

AMBASSADOR BOOKS
The Mount
2 Woodstock Link
Belfast, BT6 8DD, Northern Ireland, UK
www.ambassadormedia.co.uk

The colophon is a trademark of Ambassador

This book is dedicated to
Dr. Billy Graham
who has taught me so much about
what it really means to be undefeated through
the power of the Holy Spirit.

Dr. Don Wilton is my beloved pastor and friend.
He continues to be such a blessing to me.
Our many times of sharing together
have stimulated my mind and encouraged my spirit.
—Dr. Billy Graham

CONTENTS

THE PATHWAY TO SUCCESS

IN THE EYES OF THE world, the pathway to success is paved with power, fame, and achievement. God's Word presents a different perspective of a successful life. Does worldly success grant a person the ability to conquer life's battles, or does it contribute to those problems? You can personally achieve the kind of success that pleases God and gives you complete peace and satisfaction—even in the midst of life's battles. God's Word outlines the kind of success that trumps your dreams in your wildest imagination. With God's help, you can achieve an undefeated life!

The rags to riches story of entrepreneur Al Copeland is an example of success in the eyes of the world. Copeland was the founder of Popeye's Famous Fried Chicken and went on to establish other businesses that made him a multi-millionaire.

Copeland's life, ravaged with cancer, ended early. He died of a rare, aggressive form of cancer and at age sixty-four was laid to rest in a cemetery in Metairie, Louisiana. The newspapers teemed with details of the flamboyant graveside memorial service. Martha Carr wrote in the *Times-Picayune*:

"By twilight on Sunday, four white open-sided tents had been set up around Copeland's columned mausoleum, which was encircled by his cars, motorcycles, and a speedboat in preparation for his burial. Two monster trucks were parked near the cemetery gate, and his racing boat, with tongues of flame on each side, was behind the mausoleum. About 10 racing cars and sports cars were in a semicircle nearby, with several motorcycles between most of the cars. Included in the funeral procession were eleven white Lincoln limousines for the Copeland family.[1] Three of his four wives, five sons, four daughters, and thirteen grandchildren were present to witness the elaborate send off. "At the time of his death, Al had but two goals. The first was to find a cure for his rare cancer, and the second was to finish the boat and break the world record."[2] One can see that Al Copeland was an extraordinary man. He was extremely successful in the eyes of the world, but only God knows what was in his heart. Worldly success sometimes brings about great distress, but God's success can result in great peace and contentment even in the midst of life's battles. On the other hand, success in God's eyes can bring about success in the world as well.

I interact with people from all different walks of life in my ministry. Some people consider promotion to the top executive position of their company as success, but if they are not following God's plan, they may risk the loss of their loved ones due to excessive commitments and hyper-busyness. Rising to the top of the ladder of success does not help in

1   http://www.nola.com/news/index.ssf/2008/03/post.html.
2   http://www.seriousoffshore.com/phenomenon-takes-a-shot-at-the-record-update/.

dealing with life's problems. Earning a six-digit salary or being drafted by the NFL merits success in the eyes of the world. But these successes are of no value when one is in trouble with the law because of drugs, alcohol abuse, or criminal domestic violence. Living in an upper-class neighborhood, driving a fast motor-car, and having lots of toys are worthless when faced with a life-threatening illness.

As one who believes that God pours out blessings on His people, I certainly celebrate the many blessings of life. I know many wonderful people who continually celebrate their own blessings with thankfulness to God for His goodness. They know that material blessings cannot alleviate the challenges that life has to offer. They understand that following God in the midst of worldly success can help one maneuver through the battles of life in a successful way. However, sometimes success in the perspective of the world breeds the desire for more and more success. This rarely brings true happiness. Financial success often imprisons one like a hamster in a cage, running on a wheel, striving relentlessly for the goal but never reaching the desired destination. Acquiring millions of dollars often sparks an insatiable desire of always wanting more yet never being satisfied. Also, loneliness can be a battle that is difficult to overcome in a world of financial success. A very wealthy man once shared his feelings with me: "It is impossible for a rich man to have a true friend."

I wonder what Al Copeland would have to say about success if he could come back to this earth after having been on the other side of eternity. I believe he would stress the importance of giving one's heart and life to the Lord Jesus. I also believe he would say that love is supreme and money doesn't really matter as much as people think. I believe he would let us know time is short, and life on this earth is unsure and temporary. He would tell us that God is the most important thing in life and we should love Him supremely. He would tell us there are some things we simply cannot control, like when or how we die. He would focus completely on the Lord Jesus and His willingness to lay down His life for the sons and daughters of the world. Perhaps Mr. Copeland's boats, money, racing records, or even the critical need to find a cure for cancer, might not be of utmost importance. He would tell us to surrender completely to the Lord Jesus, because He is the only person who can rescue all people from the eternal consequences of sin. And, once having been set free from sin, the Holy Spirit will empower the believer, enabling that person to have the means to combat the challenges of life. Besides, it was the Lord Jesus who warned us not to store our treasures on earth where "moth and rust will corrupt," but, rather, to "lay up treasures in heaven where neither moth nor rust will corrupt."

In this book, we will determine what it means to have the kind of success that will help you make it through the struggles of life and will bring you peace and contentment no matter what you are facing. Success God's way will bring you great peace, knowing that you have lived your life with few regrets. There will be no shame in life nor fear in facing death.

Regardless of your age, it is never too late to start. You have a second chance until you take your final breath on this side of eternity. However, you never know when that will be. If you have never given your heart and life to the Lord Jesus Christ, I urge you to confess your sins and believe in your heart today. Romans 3:23 reads, "For all have sinned and fall short of the glory of God." Romans 10:10 explains how to be saved: "For with the heart one believes and is justified and with the mouth one confesses and is saved." Romans 10:13 explains this further: "For everyone who calls on the name of the Lord will be saved."

SUCCESS GOD'S WAY WILL BRING YOU GREAT PEACE.

Will you bow before the Lord right where you are and call on His name? He is ready and waiting to come into your heart. His Spirit will live in your heart and guide you through the rest of your days on earth. He will be your protector and teacher. He will guide you to live your life for the Lord Jesus Christ. He will give you peace and contentment no matter what may come your way. He will walk with you through the struggles of life, help you fight the battles you face, and give you joy even in the midst of a battle. Do not allow pride, riches, or worldly success to stop you from surrendering your life to Christ. Accept the Lord Jesus Christ today and begin your pathway of success to an undefeated life. If you have questions or would like to share your story, please call the number in the back of this book and talk with someone at The Encouraging Word today. You will be glad you did!

CHAPTER ONE – STUDY QUESTIONS

1. Name three worldly successes you have achieved.

_____

_____

_____

2. Have any of those successes come at a great price? If so, what has been the cost for your success?

_____

_____

_____

3. What battles are you facing in your life at the present time?

_____

_____

_____

4. Have you completely surrendered your heart and life to Jesus Christ? If so, write a brief description of your salvation experience. If you need more space, use a blank sheet of paper and then tuck it into your book here.

_____

_____

_____

5. If you have never invited Jesus to take control of your life, write a prayer asking Him to come into your heart and life today forgiving you of yours sins, and taking control of your life. This will be the first step in conquering the battles you are facing. Call the number for The Encouraging Word in the back of this book and share with someone what you have done. You will receive more information on how to grow as a Christian.

_____

_____

_____

ACHIEVING SUCCESS GOD'S WAY

STRIVING FOR SUCCESS GOD'S WAY does not mean that you cannot strive for success in your job or encourage your children to be ambitious. Nor does it mean you should not enjoy the many blessings of life. But God's perspective begins with Him. Everything good in life flows out of a personal relationship with Him. God wants you to succeed. He wants you to achieve. Out of an intimate relationship with the Lord Jesus Christ will flow spiritual character that will serve to guide your actions to successfully living an undefeated life. He is interested in your character, in who you are, because that will determine what you do. Your relationship with Christ will determine how you respond to the battles you face in life and whether you are truly successful in overcoming battles you encounter.

> **YOUR RELATIONSHIP WITH CHRIST WILL DETERMINE HOW YOU RESPOND TO THE BATTLES YOU FACE IN LIFE.**

Now that you are completely assured that you have accepted Jesus into your heart and have surrendered your life to Him, you can begin to have a daily relationship with Him. Through prayer and reading the Bible you will be able to grow in your relationship with the Lord. He is totally trustworthy and completely dependent in every way. God will never let you down. He will speak to you through His Word. He will guide you through life's journey and give you peace and comfort no matter what you are facing.

Since God is vitally interested in the totality of life, He is not only vitally interested in your actions and their outward results—He is also vitally concerned with your inner character. What does this mean? Consider the difference between *being* and *doing*. Will you follow God's strategy for success in being a person of true character inwardly? Today's society has this principle out of kilter. The world is far more interested in what you do, how much money you earn, who you know, and what position you occupy than in your thoughts, motives, and feelings toward God and other people. In many cases, the world looks at a situation and believes the end justifies the means. Many people believe they should fight their way to the top by any means possible. God, on the other hand, is more interested in *how* you accomplished the financial success in your business than He is in the amount of money you earned. Success in what you do may not be the avenue of complete and total satisfaction in life. The most lasting satisfaction and the greatest joys are produced when one's motives are pure and one's heart is clean.

True success and satisfaction can be attained on this earth, with God's help. And it is never too late to start! Begin the process right where you are today. Challenges, trouble, heartache, and sorrow will always be present in our sinful and fallen world, but you can have peace and joy regardless.

CHAPTER TWO – STUDY QUESTIONS

1. On a scale from 1 to 10, with 1 being non-existent and 10 being the best, how would you rate your relationship with Jesus Christ on a daily basis?

_____

_____

_____

2. What is your definition of success in the Christian life?

_____

_____

_____

3. What are some goals you would like to set up to improve your relationship with Jesus Christ?

_____

_____

_____

_____

4. What negatives can you honestly identify in your personal life that you need to work on?

_____

_____

_____

5. What are some characteristics you would like to develop in your life as a result of your intimate relationship with Jesus Christ?

_____

_____

_____

LIVING BY THE POWER OF GODLY PRINCIPLES

ANY EFFORT TO PAINT A picture of success for the Christian is complex. The only way it can be achieved is to understand God's blueprint. Since He created us, He knows us. And He loves us. And because He loves us, He has set standards for us to live by. Believers who follow Christ will want to follow in His footsteps. This is why we are called to a life of obedience. This is the hallmark of Christian discipleship. When we follow Him, God, by His Holy Spirit, will guide us and enable us to live out our lives according to His will. The indwelling power and presence of the Holy Spirit will provide all the means necessary to overcome life's battles. Genuine, undeniable success will be the result. You will be able to face the end of your life undefeated.

THE INDWELLING POWER AND PRESENCE OF THE HOLY SPIRIT WILL PROVIDE ALL THE MEANS NECESSARY TO OVERCOME LIFE'S BATTLES.

I believe we can have no greater example of a successful, well-lived life and ministry than that of the evangelist Dr. Billy Graham. Dr. Graham is a member of the church where I serve as Senior Pastor, and I have had the privilege of spending time with him on a weekly basis for many years now. It has been my pleasure, great honor, and blessing to sit at his feet and glean from his wisdom through the years.

I recall one day when the two of us were sitting in rocking chairs on the porch of his modest log home on the very top of a beautiful mountain in Montreat, N.C., where he and Ruth had raised their children. By this time, Ruth had already gone home to be with Jesus. Dr. Graham's body was growing old, but his mind remained sharp. On my visits we often share many hours discussing my sermon for the coming Sunday; Dr. Graham loves talking about God's Word. At other times we ask each other deep theological questions and share our thoughts. Occasionally we simply talk about our families, golf, or the weather. One thing we do each time is pray about the things on our hearts. On that particular day, I asked him a question that I had been pondering for quite some time.

"Dr. Graham, to what do you attribute the success of the Billy Graham Evangelistic Association and your life personally? You have remained faithful to the Lord Jesus Christ for ninety plus years now. You have always remained faithful to your wife and family. Your reputation has remained unmarred through the years. You are considered to be America's pastor. How do you explain your success when so many other well-known preachers and evangelists have failed miserably in their ministries, their families, and their reputations?"

Dr. Graham looked at me with his clear blue eyes and told me the following story. I will relate the story in my own words and memory of what he said that day.

In 1948, Billy Graham and three of his team members—George Beverly Shea, Grady Wilson, and Cliff Barrows—were in Modesto, California, preparing for a crusade. For some time, Dr. Graham had been concerned that many evangelists at that time were succumbing to moral and ethical failure. One afternoon while meeting together, Dr. Graham asked the three men to go back to their motel rooms and think about the history of evangelists and to write down what their pitfalls and mistakes in ministry had been; Dr. Graham would do the same. The four men agreed to pray about those issues and ask God to show them ways they could keep away from those mistakes in their own ministries. Dr. Graham asked them to make a list to compare the next day when they were to meet again. When the four men met together later, to their surprise the lists were remarkably similar. They discussed these areas and soon came up with an informal understanding between themselves. It was a shared commitment to do everything they could to uphold Biblical principles in their personal lives and ministries. This commitment had everything to do with who they were, which would affect what they would do in their lives and ministries.

The first area was integrity related to money and financial issues. These men wanted to be men who were completely honest and dependable in their dealings with people. They determined to avoid all questionable financial dealings as well as emotional appeals for money in the crusades. Instead, they would depend on the Lord to provide the necessary funds for their ministry, and He always did. In other words, they adopted the principal of **integrity.**

The second area was the danger of sexual immorality. These men adopted the principal of **purity** in relations with the opposite sex. They pledged to one another to avoid any situation that would even *appear* suspicious. And from that day on, Dr. Graham never traveled, met with, or ate alone with any woman other than his wife. The four men set up very strict guidelines for their travels, even to the point of sending someone into Dr. Graham's hotel room before he entered, to make sure no one was hiding in his room to blindside him with a scandal. They helped each other to guard against moral compromise, and as a result, God honored their personal lives and ministry.

The third area was related to the tendency of many evangelists to carry on their work apart from the local church. So these men adopted the principle of **accountability.** They agreed to be men who were accountable to God, to each other, to the people who invited them to crusades, and to their wives and families. In the years to come, the Billy Graham Evangelistic Association made it their practice to work with as many churches as possible in the areas of their crusades. These men had to be accountable and uphold their integrity if this was to be successful; they also had to be accountable to their wives and families. Ruth was an important part of

Dr. Graham's decision-making process, even though she was at home raising the children during many of those years. In a letter he wrote to her, Dr. Graham expressed his complete trust in her advice and accountability.

> Your advice is the only one that I really trust. You have no idea how often I have listened to your advice and it has been as if it were spoken from the Lord. During the past year, I have learned to lean on you a great deal more than you realize.[3]

Being accountable to your spouse is of the utmost importance in a trusting, monogamous relationship.

The fourth area was publicity. These men adopted the principle of **humility.** They agreed to strive for humility in their ministries and in their personal lives. They constantly reminded each other not to think too highly of themselves and that God is a jealous God and will not share His glory with others. Dr. Graham reminisced about often making this statement to his team: "The glory belongs to the Lord, boys! It all belongs to Him!"

These four areas—integrity, accountability, purity, and humility—became these men's core values, and they called these principles the Modesto Manifesto. They were quick to remind each other of these principles when a compromising situation would arise. Prayer was an essential part of the manifesto. In answer to their prayers, God kept the Billy Graham

---

3   Graham, Billy, *Just as I Am: The Autobiography of Billy Graham* (New York: Harper Collins, 1997), 252.

Evangelistic Association team members away from evil for more than fifty years. These principles not only helped them to be successful in their ministries but in their personal lives and families as well.

Both Mr. Shea and Mr. Wilson, so beloved by Dr. Graham, have gone on to be with the Lord. Dr. Graham and Mr. Barrows are both in their nineties at the time of this writing. All of them can face eternity with a sense of success of a life well-lived for the Lord. That is appealing to me. What about you? Would you like to face the gates of heaven with these words from the Lord Jesus: "Well done, good and faithful servant!"? (Taken from Matthew 25:23.)

Think about the four principles that Dr. Graham adopted so many years ago: integrity, honesty, purity, and humility. How are you doing in these areas of your life? Living a life of integrity, honesty, purity, and humility is impossible to do alone. You need help and strength from the Holy Spirit. Just like the Billy Graham Evangelistic Association team prayed for one another to be able to uphold these values, we must pray to the Lord for strength in our own lives.

LIVING BY GODLY PRINCIPLES GIVES YOU THE POWER TO BE SUCCESSFUL IN LIFE.

Living by godly principles gives you the power to be successful in life. If you are traveling in another state, for example, you won't have to decide whether or not you will cheat on your husband or wife: your decision will have already been made. You won't have to decide whether you will spend company money for personal use, when the occasion arises. The decision is already made, because of the godly principles you have adopted for your life.

The devil loves it when you do not live by godly principles. It is easy for him to trick you into sin. However, he does not give up just because you adopt godly principles. He then works much harder to ruin your testimony. That is why it is important to keep your eyes trained on God and live by the power of the Holy Spirit daily.

You may think of additional principles that are needed in your life, other than the four we have already mentioned. I encourage you to pray and ask the Lord to show you the principles that will be important in your life. At first you will have to *think about* living by these principles. In time, though, they will become ingrained in your thought processes so much so that you do not even think about them. The principles will become who you are, and your actions will follow suit.

In addition to setting up these principles in your life, you must determine how you will live them out on a daily basis. You must realize that life is a battlefield. Ephesians 6:12 says, "For we do not wrestle against flesh and blood, but against the rulers, against the authorities, against the cosmic powers over this present darkness, against the spiritual forces of evil in the heavenly places." It is important to understand that the only way to fight the battle is with spiritual power, not flesh and blood. I believe we can only accomplish this by establishing a strategy for living out these principles for success in our lives.

CHAPTER THREE – STUDY QUESTIONS

1. How are you doing in the area of integrity?

_____

_____

_____

2. How are you doing in the area of accountability?

_____

_____

_____

3. How are you doing in the area of purity?

_____

_____

_____

4. How are you doing in the area of humility?

_____

_____

_____

5. What are some other principles you will determine to live by in your daily life?

_____

_____

_____

FIGHTING LIFE'S BATTLES GOD'S WAY

FEW PEOPLE INHERIT SUCCESS. MANY inherit treasure, but most have to work hard to translate that treasure into success. Many a well-paid professional athlete has ended up squandering his bank balance with short notice and in a very short space of time. Proper planning, discipline, wisdom, and careful strategizing are essential to a long and prosperous life. The fruit of the tree will rot if it is not properly cultivated, handled, picked, and preserved. This metaphor can be applied to the life of all believers. The act of salvation in Christ is accompanied by the work of sanctification through the indwelling of the Spirit of Christ. Guidance comes through godly friends, pastors, teachers, and, above all, through the Word of God. The ability to fight life's battles God's way is in direct proportion to the way in which believers submit to the Lordship of Christ. In so doing, He enables us to map out a strategy designed to help us be undefeated as we face life's battles and hardships.

History books have recorded multiple examples of great and decisive victories that have been won because of careful and decisive planning. In the military field, establishing a beachhead is an important strategy for fighting the battle. A beachhead establishes a stronghold and often provides a platform from which to launch a direct offensive against the enemy. Beachheads can be seen like islands in the sea. Each island is a stepping-stone to the mainland. Great generals like General Douglas MacArthur and many others understood this principle of operation. During World War Two, it was evident that the fall of the Japanese mainland could only be achieved by the systematic dismantling of the islands that surrounded the mainland. As each was taken, a foothold was established. Each beachhead made the next one possible. It also fortified our defenses. It allowed for regrouping to take place. It closed the distance between the enemy and the conqueror.

TO BE SUCCESSFUL IN REACHING A GOAL, YOU MUST HAVE A STRATEGY.

Some very simple steps may be helpful at the start, when mapping out a strategy to overcome life's battles:

1. Pray earnestly and ask the Lord to help you engage according to His commands.

2. Read God's Word with an expectant heart and an open mind.

3. Enlist a family member or friend to partner with you in this endeavor.

4. Acknowledge your need before the Lord. Confess your sin to Him.

5.   Identify the battles you are facing in detail.

6.   Write them down in detail.

7.   Establish your step-by-step beachheads in detail.

8.   Pray over each one and define your "win."

9.   Advance in victory and confidence; if God be for you, who can be against you?

To be successful in reaching a goal, you must have a strategy or plan. I am the pastor of a church, and we have a strategy to reach our goals as a church. We prayed for two years, "Lord, give us a strategy to reach our goals." We sought help and guidance. We prayed a great deal and shared together extensively. He finally answered our prayers and we adopted the principles that govern our actions to meet our goals. We also had to set up a strategy to meet those goals. This has proved a great blessing to all as we grow in the Lord together. It has enabled us to focus on matters that really matter. It allows us to identify battles that need to be fought and battles that need to be ignored. Not everything the devil brings to the table warrants a response. Sometimes all he tries to do is get God's people to hit back. And most of the time when we hit back, we do so in a manner that displeases the Lord and ends up making the battle even worse. There are times when all God wants us to do is take our hands off and hand it all to Him. In the battlefields of life, He is the greatest commanding officer ever.

In the same way, you must have a strategy based on the godly principles you live by. In your professional life, the company which employs you should have a business strategy. If you own a business, you should have one. What about your personal life? Do you have a life strategy based on the principles by which you live?

In 2 Chronicles chapters 17–20 we find the story of Jehoshaphat, king of Judah, who lived in Jerusalem. The Bible says he was God's man. In 2 Chronicles 17:3 we see that the Lord was with Jehoshaphat because he walked in the ways of his father David. He did not worship the false gods around him, but sought the God of his father and walked by His commands. He was God's man for that time. So the Lord established the kingdom in his hand, and all of Judah brought tribute to Jehoshaphat, which resulted in his having great riches and honor.

As time went on, Jehoshaphat grew stronger and built fortresses and storage cities. He had thousands of fighting men who were brave warriors. The Lord led Jehoshaphat to devise a plan—a strategy—for his officials to instruct the people from the book of the Lord's instruction. This strategy may seem a little strange in this day and time, but from it we can find a strategy for fighting the battles we face in our own lives. God's Word was relevant in Jehoshaphat's day and it is equally relevant in our day.

In 2 Chronicles 20, Jehoshaphat was facing a great enemy. The Moabites and the Ammonites, together with some of the

Meunites, came to fight against Jehoshaphat and his people. A vast number from beyond the Dead Sea had gathered at En Gedi, and Jehoshaphat was afraid. He resolved to seek the Lord for instructions, because the enemy was closing in quickly on his people. When Jehoshaphat sought help from the Lord, God gave to him a strategy.

The twentieth chapter of 2 Chronicles is the account of Jehoshaphat's victory. In response to the vast army that was coming from the Dead Sea to attack, Jehoshaphat proclaimed a fast for all of Judah so they could pray and ask God what they must do. All of the men, women, and children stood before the Lord. As they fasted and prayed, the Spirit of the Lord came upon Jahaziel, the son of Zachariah. Jahaziel spoke words to all of the people encouraging them not to be afraid or discouraged. He told them the battle was not theirs; it belonged to the Lord. He encouraged them to stand firm, hold their position, and see the salvation of the Lord on their behalf. Jahaziel finished with, "Go out tomorrow, and the Lord will be with you."

At this, Jehoshaphat bowed with his face to the ground and all the people of Judah and Jerusalem fell down and worshipped God. The next morning they rose early and went out into the wilderness of Tekoa. Jehoshaphat counseled the people to believe in God and trust Him. He appointed certain people to sing to the Lord and praise Him in holy attire as they advanced in front of the army.

When they began to sing, the Lord set an ambush against the men who were coming to fight against Jehoshaphat. The men of Ammon and the men of Moab fought together against the inhabitants of Mount Seir and destroyed their whole army. Then an amazing thing happened. The Ammonites and Moabites turned on one another and destroyed each other. When Jehoshaphat and the people of Judah came to the watchtower of the wilderness, all they could do was stand and gaze at the dead bodies lying on the ground. The Lord had fought the battle for them. All that remained for them to do was collect the goods, clothing, and precious things. They took as much as they could, until they could carry no more. In verses 27–30 we see the end of the story:

> Then, led by Jehoshaphat, all the men of Judah and Jerusalem returned joyfully to Jerusalem, for the Lord had given them cause to rejoice over their enemies. They entered Jerusalem and went to the temple of the Lord with harps and lutes and trumpets. . . . The fear of God came upon all the kingdoms of the countries when they heard how the Lord had fought against the enemies of Israel. And the kingdom of Jehoshaphat was at peace; for his God had given him rest on every side. (NIV)

Jehoshaphat was facing a real dilemma. He had a vast army coming against him and he had no idea what he should do. Second Chronicles 20 outlines the strategy for his success in fighting the battle. Have you ever felt like you had a vast army coming against you in some area of your life? It is wonderful to know that this same strategy Jehoshaphat used also applies to your life in fighting the battles you face on a daily basis. Do you need help in overcoming the battles you are facing? The best way to overcome is to allow God to fight those battles for you. But there are steps you must take in order to summon God's help.

HAVE YOU EVER FELT LIKE YOU HAD A VAST ARMY COMING AGAINST YOU?

Second Chronicles 20 outlines ten steps for fighting the battles of life successfully. These ten steps are:

1. Recognize the enemy.

2. Listen to alarms.

3. Resolve to fast and pray.

4. Assemble a team.

5. Know your role: leader or follower.

6. Listen to godly counsel.

7. Attack from the front.

8. Take up your position.

9. Let worship lead.

10. Be at peace.

These steps will help you live a life of integrity, purity, accountability, and humility. God will help you conquer the enemies in your life and overcome the battles you face. The assurance that God has "got your back" will remove any fear you may have in facing these battles head-on.

I hope it is comforting to know that you do not have to fight your battles on your own. The Lord will fight them for you if you trust Him and obey His Word. I pray that God will speak to you through His Word as you read carefully the steps outlined in the following chapters. In conclusion, we must remember to thank the Lord for His goodness and to celebrate His victory in and through us.

CHAPTER FOUR – STUDY QUESTIONS

1.   Name the greatest battle you are facing right now in your life.

_____

_____

_____

2.   How have you fought your battles in the past?

_____

_____

_____

3.   Who is the real enemy in your life?

_____

_____

_____

4. Write a prayer below asking God to show you how to set up a beachhead in your life. Ask Him to show you what steps you must take in order to conquer the enemy in your life.

_____

_____

_____

CHAPTER FIVE

STEP ONE: RECOGNIZE THE ENEMY

THE FIRST STEP ON THE pathway to successfully conquering our battles is so very important, because it is extremely difficult to counter an unknown enemy. The epic battle we read about in 2 Chronicles 20:3 leaves us with no doubt that Jehoshaphat knew who his enemy was, "for real." Spiritual warfare is a real thing. The devil is alive and he is working all around us. He wants to destroy everything God has given to us, including our marriages, our children, and ultimately our very lives. He will use every means at his disposal, including pawns, to do so. A pawn is a person whom the devil uses to do his dirty work and to accomplish his goal. A pawn can also be an object or activity the devil uses to do his dirty work. The devil will use pawns in your life such as pornography, the Internet, alcohol, drugs, and greed to bring you down. He will also use a friend, an enemy, or family member who will tempt you emotionally or physically to accomplish his goal. And the church is no exception.

God has given us two fundamental institutions for our support and success in life: the family and the Church. God has ordained the family as the foundational institution of human society. He has ordained the Church as the body of Christ. The body of Christ is made up of all those throughout history who have accepted Jesus Christ as their personal Savior. Both the family and the Church are under severe attack in America and around the world. Divorce is at an all-time high and many couples see no need to actually get married. Alternative lifestyles are being hoisted up as the norms of an accepting society, regardless of any biblical mandate to the contrary. The church is disintegrating and floundering at an alarming rate. In many cases, people now seek opportunities to "go to church" without actually having to worship God or praise the name of the Lord Jesus Christ. Satan knows that if he can destroy churches and families, then he can own the world. Satan will go to any length to destroy and separate these two institutions. He will go to any lengths to destroy our churches and people who are faithful to the Lord Jesus Christ. But the devil will not succeed when confronted God's way. Be reminded that it was Jesus who said, "The gates of hell will not prevail against my church." With God's help you can live an undefeated life.

The Bible says in 1 Peter 5:8, "Be sober-minded; be watchful. Your adversary the devil prowls around like a roaring lion, seeking someone to devour." Growing up in Africa, I have seen more lions in the bush than I care to remember. I believe that lions are one of the most dangerous animals alive, because they are cunning and sly. They can move through the bush without cracking a twig and will strike before you know what has happened. When the devil begins to prowl . . . watch out! If you are in his sights, he will bring you down in a flash if you let your guard down for a second.

When God speaks to your heart and you are ready to mean business with Him, never forget who your enemy is. The Bible tells us that Jehoshaphat understood there was a vast army coming against him. This was no small matter. The enemy was no frivolous joke. Jehoshaphat was very serious about this, because he faced a serious threat. Remember, the enemy is the devil and he will use anyone or anything to trick you into sin. Always be alert and never let your guard down. Live as far away from sin as you possibly can by living as close in obedience to Christ as you can. When you spend time reading God's Word, praying, and surrounding yourself with godly people, you will have a measuring stick to go by. When you put godly behavior and actions in front of you, then you will recognize ungodly behavior and actions when they appear. Be alert and pray continually that God will protect you from pawns in your life.

Spiritual warfare is real and the true enemy is the devil. You can rest assured that God has already defeated the enemy. To remain undefeated in the battles of life, you must trust God and live in obedience to Him. The good news—God has already won the war!

CHAPTER FIVE – STUDY QUESTIONS

1. Write your description of a pawn. What are some possible pawns the devil might use in your life to trip you up and cause you to sin?

_____

_____

_____

2. It is easy to look at others as being our enemy. Read Ephesians 6:12 and write below who the real enemy is in your life.

_____

_____

_____

3. What do you think it means to live far from sin and close to Christ? What does that look like in the life of a Christian?

_____

_____

_____

4. What steps can you take to be alert against spiritual attacks?

_____

_____

_____

CHAPTER SIX

STEP TWO: LISTEN TO ALARMS

THIS SECOND STEP IS SO important to recognize. Just as the Lord provides for every need as we journey through life, so it is that He continually warns us of impending danger. He will use whatever means He chooses to do so. This is what happened to Jehoshaphat, as we read in verse three, "Alarmed, Jehoshaphat resolved to inquire of the Lord." Sometimes these alarms are obvious, like that mild run-in with the Law, or that serious discussion with your doctor, or that failure to pass that test, or that gentle voice of love that comes from your spouse. Sometimes these warnings are openly obvious, like that car crash when you had "one too many," or that preacher's voice on Sunday that stepped on your toes, or that financial struggle you continually find yourself in because you will not obey God's instructions to tithe ten percent of your income to your church. If the devil can get you to be unfaithful in your marriage, to cheat on your income taxes, to rob God of His money, and to watch that pornography—he has got you! I have found that God warns me through His Word, through my wife's loving correction, through the counsel of godly friends, through circumstances I encounter, and through the small voice of His Spirit who knocks and nudges at my heart's door. Because I belong to Jesus, I just know when something is not right. There are many occasions when I do not need rocket science to tell me I am being led by the devil. What's wrong according to God's Word is wrong. It is sin. And it has no good end. The devil will use whatever he can to break you down. He is the great deceiver, the master manipulator. He is the master thief, bar none. He sneaks around like a slithering reptile. He lurks and prowls. He is cunning and wants to destroy you.

So listen to the warnings. Do not turn your back on spiritual alarms. God puts them there for a purpose. Do not cover them up or sweep them under the rug. Be alert!

God often gives spiritual warning signs to parents in regards to their children. Parents may notice a change in the attitude or behavior of their son or daughter. They may notice a change in the friends their child hangs out with who may not be a positive influence. God gives a warning in the parent's heart that some kind of intervention is needed. Do not ignore the warning signs. But be wise in your actions. Don't bash your child's friends. Simply teach your child truth from God's Word and pray for God to change their hearts. Parents have shared with me often how they were awakened in the middle of the night and felt alarm in their hearts about their children. We must do as Jehoshaphat did. Resolve to ask God for help. Many times I have gotten out of my bed and prayed for my children. I didn't know why I woke up feeling alarmed. I simply cried out to God on their behalf.

God will sound alarms in your marriage as well. You will see things that do not quite add up, though they may seem small. Just like your home security system sounds an alarm when there is an intruder in your home, there are alarms that sound when there is an intruder in your marriage. Just as you would never ignore your home security alarm, you would be wise not to ignore alarms in your marriage as well. An intruder in your marriage could be a person of the opposite sex who is too friendly with your spouse or you. On the other hand, it could be a friend of the same sex who is pulling you away from your family by encouraging you to go out and leave your family at home too often. Your work can take on the role of the intruder in your marriage. The alarm comes when your spouse gives you those little hints that should sound an alarm in your heart and mind. An alarm might be a subtle comment by your spouse such as, "Please come home and have dinner with the family tonight. The children miss you, and I do too." Learn to recognize intruders in your marriage and listen to those alarms even though they may be indirect. Intruders are not only people; they can be things as well. Drugs, alcohol, excessive texting or social media, excessively watching sports or soap operas, and pornography can all be intruders in your marriage. Alarms will sound when these intruders enter. Listen to them and learn to set boundaries when there are intruders in your life and family. Boundaries are healthy and provide protection.

BE ALERT TO THE WARNING SIGNS GOD BRINGS ACROSS YOUR PATH.

Beware, because little things become big things. Deal with alarms immediately when the Lord Jesus brings them into your heart. For instance, dealing with anger is an issue that people often ignore. The Bible says, "Do not go to sleep on your anger." Why? Because if you go to sleep on your anger, you will wake up the next morning and your anger will have doubled. One of the reasons it will have doubled is that one cannot sleep properly when angry. And as we know from experience, a sleepless person can become an angry person.

Sometimes alarms will ring through godly people who will speak to you. Sometimes alarms will ring when you are reading the Bible. God's Word will instruct you in your mind and heart. Often alarms will ring when you are praying. God will speak to your heart and warn you of dangers in your life or the lives of others who are close to you. Be alert to the warning signs God brings across your path and allow the Lord to lead you in the right way. Jehoshaphat was alarmed and the Bible says he "resolved to inquire of the Lord, and he proclaimed a fast." When alarms come in your life, ask the Lord what you should do.

CHAPTER SIX – STUDY QUESTIONS

1. Write about an alarm you overlooked in the past. How did that affect your life?

_____

_____

_____

2. Is there an alarm in your life now that you need to pay closer attention to? What decisions do you need to make regarding that alarm?

_____

_____

_____

3. Write a prayer to God asking Him to help you be more in tune with His leading in your life. Ask Him to protect your mind and heart against evil things that can destroy your life.

_____

_____

_____

CHAPTER SEVEN

STEP THREE: RESOLVE TO FAST AND PRAY

IN MANY WAYS AND FOR many reasons, this third step could be the most important of all the steps. Without prayer, you and I are rendered helpless and hopeless. Nothing great will happen outside of prayer. The famous preacher and evangelist R.A. Torrey once said, "The reason why many fail in battle is because they wait until the hour of battle. The reason why others succeed is because they have gained their victory on their knees long before the battle came. Anticipate your battles; fight them on your knees before temptation comes, and you will always have victory."[4] In 2 Chronicles 20:3 the Bible reads, "Then Jehoshaphat was afraid and set his face to seek the Lord, and proclaimed a fast throughout all Judah." Jehoshaphat anticipated his battle, and immediately resolved to fight the battle on his knees by declaring a fast for all the people. Fasting and prayer are essential strategic ingredients in fighting the battles you will face.

---

4   R. A. Torrey, as quoted on BeliefNet, http://www.beliefnet.com/ Quotes/Evangelical/R/R-A-Torrey/The-Reason-Why-Many-Fail-In-Battle-Is-Because-They.aspx/.

WITHOUT PRAYER, YOU AND I ARE RENDERED HELPLESS AND HOPELESS.

Fasting prepares your heart and mind for prayer. Prayer produces a change in your heart that prepares you to receive the blessing that God sends your way. Otherwise, you could possibly become arrogant and prideful when God answers your prayers and blesses you. Fasting and prayer will help you know God's will for your life. It will take your focus off the things of the world and put your focus on God and spiritual things. You will have a deeper intimate relationship with God when you devote yourself to fasting and prayer. You will find help in times of trouble. You will find strength for victory over sin and temptation. It will guide you in particular situations to a godly solution.

Spiritual fasting is voluntarily giving up your physical nourishment in order to receive spiritual nourishment. Fasting involves not eating in order to focus on prayer and a deeper relationship with God. You are able to focus on the Father more in depth when you are not focusing on the things of daily life.

It is beneficial to develop a strategy for fasting before you begin. Preparing to fast will help you to be more successful in your time of fasting. Consider the following if you are planning to fast.

- Ask God to direct you in the type of fast you will do.

- If you have health issues, you will be wise to consult your physician before beginning a food fast of any length or kind.

- Confess your sins to God and open your heart to receive God's blessings. When turning from your sins, you will find that it is easier to turn toward God.

There are many different biblical ways to fast. Fasting does not necessarily mean you suddenly stop eating for days. You can declare a spiritual fast, and it may be for one day. It may be for one meal every day, for a set amount of time. It may be for two days or it could be forty days, like Jesus did. During a fast, determine to devote yourself to prayer and supplication and not focus on satisfying your physical needs. Set aside the time you would normally spend eating a meal to prayer. You may choose to find a place that you can be completely alone with God with no distractions. At other times you may choose to pray with others who are like-minded and are praying for the same things. It does not really matter if you are alone or praying with someone, the important thing is that you discipline yourself to pray. When you sincerely mean business with God, and submit to depriving your body so you can focus more completely on the Savior, God moves into your life in an extraordinary way. When you shift your focus away from the things of the world toward God, He can work in your heart and life. Fasting and prayer is an important area of the Christian life that is often neglected. James 5:16 says, "The prayer of a righteous person is powerful and effective" (NIV).

People often fast to seek God's calling on their lives. If you have never fasted, I encourage you to do so. Ask God what He wants you to do. What do you need to ask God to do in your life and in the lives of those whom you love? Fast and pray about the issues in your life, your family, your job, your health, or strongholds. Do you need a miracle? A miracle is something that only God can do. Fast and pray to prepare for times of spiritual renewal. Charles Finney, the great revivalist of the 1800s, once said, "Prayer produces such a change in us and fulfills such conditions as renders it consistent for God to do as it would not be consistent for him to do otherwise."[5] In simpler words, prayer changes you in such a way that God can do amazing work in your life that He could not do otherwise.

When you begin to fast, you may want to keep a journal and write in it while you are praying or after you finish praying. This will help you know how God is working in your life, and then you can go back and see how God has helped you overcome your battles. When you decide to fast and pray, choose an accountability partner of the same gender, or your spouse. Reveal your plan to your accountability partner, meet to talk about your progress, and pray for one another. Your accountability partner will bring an outside perspective and help you be able to see how God is working in your life.

Fasting will change you, by bringing out the things that control you. Richard Foster says in his book, *Celebration of Discipline,* "We cover up what is inside us with food and other good things, but when fasting, these things surface. If pride controls us, it will surface during fasting. At first we will rationalize that our anger is due to our hunger; then we will

---

5   Charles Finney, *Lectures on Revivals of Religion* (New York: Fleming Revell, 1868), 49, from the Christian Classics Ethereal Library, http://www.ccel.org/ccel/finney/revivals.iii.iv.html.

realize that we are angry because the spirit of anger is within us. We can rejoice in this knowledge because we know that healing is available through the power of Christ."[6] In Psalm 69:10 King David proclaimed, "When I wept and humbled my soul with fasting, it became my reproach." Fasting reveals the negatives in your heart, and then prayer can bring victory over those sinful emotions.

Fast and pray for guidance in particular situations you are facing. God will work miracles in accordance to His will. He will do for you what you cannot do for yourself. When you become serious through fasting and praying in order to be obedient to God, He will step in and fight the battle for you. When you fast and pray, you are becoming a part of something that only God can do.

---

6   Richard Foster, *Celebration of Discipline: The Pathway to Spiritual Growth* (New York: Harper Collins, 1998), 55.

CHAPTER SEVEN – STUDY QUESTIONS

1. What enemy do you have that is coming against you? Are you willing to fast and pray in order to overcome this enemy?

_____

_____

_____

2. If the answer was yes, set a plan for fasting. If you have special needs or an illness, please consult your physician before deciding to fast. Confess your sins and open your heart to receive God's blessings. Pray and ask God how you will fast. You may choose the following options. Check the one you believe God is leading you to do.

- Fast from one meal per day

- Fast one day per week

- Fast for 21 days (the Daniel Fast; for more info see www.daniel-fast.com)

- Fast for 40 days like Jesus did. Start out slow if you have never fasted before. Drink vegetable or fruit juice to get your body accustomed to being without food. Try a few days before you jump into a full forty-day fast.

_____

_____

_____

3. Plan a time to focus on prayer and reading your Bible without distractions every day.
When will you do this?
Where?

_____

_____

_____

4. Ask your spouse or someone of the same gender to be your accountability partner. Reveal your plan, meet for progress, and pray for one another. Write the name of the person you plan to ask.

_____

_____

_____

CHAPTER EIGHT

STEP FOUR: ASSEMBLE A TEAM

AS CHRISTIANS, WE NEED EACH other. Working together in unity and for one purpose is of the utmost importance in overcoming battles we face in our Christian lives. This is the picture we are given as the people of Judah contemplated the battlefield before them. 2 Chronicles 20:4 reads, "The people of Judah came together to seek help from the Lord." What a beautiful picture! Most of us can list the names of many people who have meant the world to us at various times and in numerous ways. Part of God's plan for His children is that they be surrounded with like-minded people. This is one reason the church is critical to our lives as believers. And we all need one another. It is impossible to live our lives without the help of others. The Billy Graham team held each other accountable for their core values and Dr. Graham attributes their success in having a ministry of integrity to that very thing. This truth applies to you in your marriage, your relationships, and your church.

**PART OF GOD'S PLAN FOR HIS CHILDREN
IS THAT THEY BE SURROUNDED
WITH LIKE-MINDED PEOPLE.**

Think about all the people who are important in your life—family, friends, co-workers, pastor, church, neighbors, tax accountant, dry cleaner, and grocer. We cannot live successful lives without these people.

I often refer to Jim Collins's thought-provoking book, *Good to Great.* Writing in the context of business principles, Collins says that it is imperative to get the right people on the bus and the wrong people off the bus.[7] The same ideas apply to our daily lives.

You must get the right people on the bus. We must know who should be involved in our lives and who should not. Our close relationships and associations should be chosen carefully. Close, intimate relationships with people of the opposite sex other than your spouse are risky and could pose a problem if you want to be a person who lives an obedient life to the Lord. Choose people of good character. Some people have the ability to recognize good character right away. Others are blindsided by people who *seem* to be people of good character but later turn out otherwise. Be careful in choosing people to lead you. Choose people who lead you to Christ, not away from Him. Be careful not to become dependent on a person; it is critical to only be dependent on Christ. Ask God to bring people into your life who can lead you in a closer relationship with Christ. There is a strategic place in your life for people who are not living close to the Lord or who may not know Him at all. They should never be allowed into a place of influence in your life,

---

7   Taken from *Good to Great,* by Jim Collins (New York: Harper Collins, 2001).

but should be in a place to be influenced by you. The only relationship a Christian should have with a non-Christian is to show the love of Christ that will draw that person into a loving relationship with Him. This is done through a loving and guiding relationship. If a relationship comes to the point that the other person is influencing you away from Christ, you have the wrong person on your bus.

You must get the people on your bus in the right seats. Relationships must be prioritized. Each person must be in the proper position. You cannot put a friend in the seat where a family member should sit. A co-worker or friend cannot be allowed to sit in the seat of a spouse. You also must find the right seat for yourself. You cannot put yourself or someone else in the driver's seat. That seat belongs only to Christ.

You must get the wrong people off of the bus. If there is a person in your life who influences you in the wrong way, you must get them off of the bus. If you find you are becoming attracted to or overly dependent on someone of the opposite sex who is not your spouse, you must get them off of your bus. Allowing that person to stay on your bus will cause problems in your marriage, in your personal life, and in your spiritual life. Regarding relationships with the opposite sex, I once heard a wise person say, "If you are becoming close to a person of the opposite sex who is not your spouse, don't remain close enough, long enough, for their rosebush to grow up your trellis." In thinking about that statement, I wondered just how fast a climbing rosebush would grow, so I did some research. In talking to friends who are experts on roses, I found out that roses can grow up to eight feet in one season. If left unattended, they will grow out of control. This analogy seems to be a wise warning to all of us.

Other relationships may not be adulterous but can be complicated and problematic. If a person (even of the same sex) causes conflict and draws you away from your family or influences you to sin, then you must set boundaries in that relationship. Gossip, negative talk, partying, going out with the guys or the girls and leaving your family at home too often is a red flag in a relationship. We all need those times of fellowship with friends, but balance is the key. Set boundaries so that you are spending the appropriate time alone with your spouse and appropriate family time unhindered by outsiders.

When we are influenced by others to be involved in activities or situations that are not becoming to a Christian, we must draw a line in the sand and not cross it. It is okay to invite that person on the right side of the line with you, but if they choose to cross the line in the wrong direction, you must get them off the bus. This is often a difficult decision. It can be uncomfortable to break off a relationship, but it will be easier if you make a decision to obey God and stick to it. When you decide to be obedient to God, often times people who are not willing to obey God will make the separation naturally. If you choose not to participate in their activities, gossip, and ungodly plans, they will most likely choose to move on without you.

Occasionally, I have people ask me if their spouse could be the wrong person. This is a tough question, but the Bible is clear in the answer. Sometimes a person will make a decision to marry someone without really knowing the person well enough. Their spouse may be deceitful in saying they are a Christian and later admits that they are not. Sometimes a person will marry and their feelings of love will dwindle with every hurt or offense. Are any of these reasons to kick your spouse off of the bus? According to God's Word, none of these are good reasons. When you take your marriage vows before God, it is a done deal. God's design for marriage is one man with one woman for a lifetime. First Peter 3:1–2, 7 clarifies the importance of one's conduct toward their spouse. Verses 1–2 speak about the wife's responsibility: "Likewise, wives, be subject to your own husbands, so that even if some do not obey the word, they may be won without a word by the conduct of their wives, when they see your respectful and pure conduct." Verse 7 speaks to husbands: "Likewise, husbands, live with your wives in an understanding way, showing honor to the woman as the weaker vessel, since they are heirs with you of the grace of life, so that your prayers may not be hindered."

You must put the right person in the driver's seat. Allowing Christ to lead your life is the most important decision you can make. He is Lord, no matter what you do or say. Are you willing to allow Him to direct your life? He can do whatever He pleases, but often He gives you a choice. You can submit to His authority or you can take control yourself. When you put yourself in the driver's seat, inevitably you will go down a one-way street the wrong way. We often feel competent to drive our bus. We want to sit on the throne that rightly belongs to Him. The only driver who has the license and ability to drive is the Lord Jesus. Can you imagine a bus filled with people without a driver or an unqualified driver? When you surrender your life to Him, He will steer you in the right direction.

You do not have to be alone in what you are going through. God will lead you to the right team if you ask Him, and He will fight the battle for you.

CHAPTER EIGHT – STUDY QUESTIONS

1. Name the people whom you believe are on your team.

_____

_____

_____

2. Is there a person you believe to be in the wrong seat? If so, how can you put that person in the right seat?

_____

_____

_____

3. Is there a person you believe should not be on your bus? If so, write a plan to get that person off your bus. Ask God to lead you in this plan. If you have any reservations, then before taking an action, share your plan with a godly person whom you can trust.

_____

_____

_____

4. Be honest with yourself to determine if God is in the driver's seat of your bus. If He is not, write a prayer asking Him to take control of your life today.

_____

_____

_____

STEP FIVE: KNOW YOUR ROLE

THE FIFTH STEP CAN SOMETIMES cause contention, but it is vitally important when facing the battles of life as a believer. Should you lead or follow when facing a battle? It is important to understand which position you are to assume at different points in your life. Sometimes God plans for you to lead, and other times He plans for you to follow. When you live close to the Lord, read His Word and pray, He will speak to your heart and you will know His will.

Jehoshaphat proved that leading by example is the best way to lead. If you lead and no one follows, you are not really leading. If you tell others what to do and are not doing it yourself, you are still not leading. Verse 18 reads, "Jehoshaphat bowed his head with his face to the ground, and all Judah and the inhabitants of Jerusalem fell down before the Lord, worshipping the Lord." Jehoshaphat led the way by example and the others followed him in worshipping God. Verse 20 reads, "And they rose early in the morning and went out into the wilderness of Tekoa. And when they went out, Jehoshaphat stood and said, "Hear me, Judah and inhabitants of Jerusalem! Believe in the Lord your God and you will be established; believe his prophets and you will succeed. And when he had taken counsel with the people, he appointed those who were to sing to the Lord and praise him in holy attire, as they went before the army." Jehoshaphat was the appointed leader. He rose to the occasion and went out with his people. He didn't send them out, he went out with them. Then he stood and took charge, and appointed those who were to sing. The Bible doesn't tell us that anyone opposed his command, even though it didn't seem to be the most logical thing to do at the moment. They apparently trusted his leadership. I believe they trusted him because of his reputation. He had proven himself to be trustworthy because of his faithfulness and walk with God. Second Chronicles 17:3–6 affirms the reasons why they trusted him: "The Lord was with Jehoshaphat, because he walked in the earlier ways of his father David. He did not seek the Baals, but sought the God of his father and walked in his commandments, and not according to the practices of Israel. Therefore the Lord established the kingdom in his hand. And all Judah brought tribute to Jehoshaphat, and he had great riches and honor. His heart was courageous in the ways of the Lord. And furthermore, he took the high places and the Asherim out of Judah." Jehoshaphat was faithful to God and had no other gods before Him. Because of that, the Lord was with him.

LEADING BY EXAMPLE IS THE BEST WAY TO LEAD.

Being a spiritual leader sets a person up to a higher level of accountability before God. We are all accountable to God for our actions, but leaders are held to a stricter judgment. James 3:1 says, "Not many of you should become teachers, my brothers, for you know that we who teach will be judged with greater strictness."

Whether you are leading or following, there are important issues to consider. If you are leading, you must be obedient to God and lead by a godly example. If you are following, you must look for a person to follow who is obedient to God and leads by a godly example. When you are seeking God's presence through prayer and fasting, you will recognize those qualities in the person you are seeking to follow. When you are seeking God's presence through prayer and fasting, you will exhibit those qualities to those who will follow you.

Ask God to show you today if you are to lead or follow in working through the life battle you are facing at the moment. He will guide you every step of the way.

CHAPTER NINE – STUDY QUESTIONS

1. Can you think of a situation when God chose you to lead in a situation that you had to completely depend on Him for guidance? If so, write below how God brought you through.

_____

_____

_____

2. Can you think of a situation when you had to follow someone else's leadership? If so, explain the difficulties you faced in following, or explain the joys in following a person who trusted God to lead.

_____

_____

_____

3. Write a prayer to God asking Him to show you what to do about a difficult time you are facing now.

_____

_____

_____

CHAPTER TEN

STEP SIX: LISTEN TO GODLY COUNSEL

ONE OF THE MOST DIFFICULT tasks in life, for most people, is to listen while someone else talks. We all talk a great deal, and some of us more than others. But we are less inclined to listen. And we seldom listen to the wisdom of those God has set to guide us spiritually. The issues facing the people of Judah were painfully evident. They were in trouble and were facing a vast army. The likelihood of their demise was a real possibility. But God had a plan. He always does. And an integral part of His plan was to funnel His will and His way through His appointed leader. Jehoshaphat was the king and he was the leader. He was the one God had called to lead, to set up the beachhead, but God chose to speak His counsel through one of Jehoshaphat's men. This is an amazing fact. Jehoshaphat was king, but he listened to another man speak God's wisdom.

GOD ALWAYS HAS A PLAN.

We see the account in 2 Chronicles 20:13–18. Verses 13–14 say, "Meanwhile all Judah stood before the Lord, with their little ones, their wives, and their children. And the Spirit of the Lord came upon Jahaziel." The following verse continues, "Listen, all Judah and inhabitants of Jerusalem and King

Jehoshaphat: Thus says the Lord to you, 'Do not be afraid and do not be dismayed at this great horde, for the battle is not yours but God's.'" Then Jahaziel continued to describe what would happen and what they were to do as a result.

Is it not amazing that it was not Jehoshaphat speaking? It is a foolish leader who does not understand that the greatest leaders in the world are the greatest servants in the world. The greatest hallmark of spiritual leadership is servanthood. As a leader, God will surround you with men and women who are unbelievably wise in their leadership and their godly counsel. Listen to them. Jehoshaphat listened to Jahaziel, whose advice came directly from the Lord God, and it certainly paid off in the end.

THE GREATEST LEADERS IN THE WORLD ARE THE GREATEST SERVANTS IN THE WORLD.

How do you know if the counsel you receive is indeed godly counsel? What is the measuring stick to be used to decide if someone is giving godly counsel or if the devil is just trying to get you off track? Here are a few guidelines that will help you.

- Is this person a growing Christian who makes godly personal decisions?

- Is this person emotionally stable displaying good character?

- Does this person's counsel line up with the Bible? If not, you can be assured that God would not tell you to make a decision that conflicted with His Word.

- Is this person a good leader in his or her own family?

- Does this person live out the advice he gives to others?

- Is he or she tried and tested? What do others say about this person?

Sometimes the answers to questions and decisions you are making are cut and dried. The Bible is clear about them. There is no gray area. Those decisions are easy, and godly counsel is just a matter of confirmation that you should do the right thing. On the other hand, sometimes the Bible is not clear on specific situations and there is not a clear cut right or wrong decision. There is more than one possible decision that would be neither wrong nor ungodly. It is simply a matter of what you would prefer or what would be the wisest decision for that particular situation. The battle strategy for your life is quite important, and God will put godly people in your life who can advise you in the right direction. The people you choose for confidants or to give you advice should be trusted people whom you know and respect. They should be carefully chosen due to their godly track record.

The beauty of this whole idea of godly counsel is connected to the unity of God's people. There is power in becoming a team of people who work together for one purpose. That purpose is to serve and glorify God in all we do. God puts people together who complement one another in their personalities, their strengths and weaknesses, and in their talents. When individuals come together as one unit striving for the same goal, each doing his or her own job, there will be power and impact like you have never seen before. Even though Jehoshaphat was the ultimate leader, he depended on Jahaziel for godly counsel. Because Jehoshaphat humbled himself and did not let pride get in his way, the Lord fought the battle and they won a mighty victory.

CHAPTER TEN – STUDY QUESTIONS

1.   Write a brief description of a time when you were given unwise counsel. What should you have done differently?

_____

_____

_____

2.   Name the characteristics of a person whom you should seek counsel from.

_____

_____

_____

3.   How can you know for sure if you are receiving godly counsel from a person?

_____

_____

_____

STEP SEVEN: ATTACK FROM THE FRONT

WHEN WE LOOK AT THE counsel Jahaziel gave to King Jehoshaphat, it is obvious that he is laying out the battle strategy. "Tomorrow, march down against them." If I were a military analyst, I could perhaps map out this battle plan for you, but you can imagine a vast army coming against them from Edom. I have been to this area, so I can picture it in my mind. I have been to this battleground. The mountains of the Ammonites stretch out beautifully across the horizon and the valley below is massive. When Jehoshaphat topped the mountain, he looked down through the valley and saw an overwhelming force marching across the valley. Jahaziel comes to the king and basically says, "You need to attack him from the front. Do not go and hide behind the other side of the hill; rally your men together and march down and meet them there—face to face."

Here is the bottom line. When faced with an obvious enemy attack, deal with the problem head-on. It seldom helps to sidestep the issue or to pamper the problem. The devil is never nice, and he has no consideration or kindness. Remember, he is out to rob and kill and destroy. He wants to take it all away from you and, most of all, he wants to discredit the Lord our God.

I am not saying that you should literally, physically, attack other people if you have an issue with them. There is a proper way to respond when there is a problem between you and another person. A good example of this in life is if you have a problem with your husband or wife. Talk directly, up front, face to face. Innuendos, feelings, and suggestions do not work. If you have conflict in your life, deal with it up front, face to face. This is one of the things I love about my wife. She does not play emotional games with me. If she is hurt or irritated, we sit down, talk about it face to face, solve the problem, and then we go on enjoying our life together.

If something inappropriate is going on in your church, do not go around and gossip to people who are not involved in the situation. Go straight to the source, and expect the same from others. Do not beat around the bush.

Often when people face struggles, whether in their church, in their marriage, or in relationships with family, friends, or co-workers, by nature they sulk around feeling hurt. They skirt around the issue and the problem drags on. Everyone knows there is an elephant in the room, but no one will mention it. When someone hurts you, the best way to deal with it is directly, but with respect and kindness. Stand up courageously and deal with it. Make your decisions based on God's Word. We don't need to call a council meeting. We don't need to get on the phone and gossip like so many people do. Gossip is destructive. Do not allow this kind of behavior to creep into your life. It is important to be direct when you are doing the Lord's work. You can do this tactfully, but do not try to go in the back door when dealing with your family or brothers and sisters in Christ.

In facing the battles of life with our brothers and sisters in Christ, the Bible is clear. In Matthew 18:15, Jesus says, "If your brother sins against you, go and tell him his fault, between you and him alone. If he listens to you, you have gained your brother." Pray and fast before going into this kind of meeting, as did Jehoshaphat and his people. Genuinely pray for the person and the situation. Pray for wisdom and guidance in dealing with the person. Set up a time to talk—don't blindside the person in the hallway at church. Sit down and talk like two grown adults and make sure there are no childish ways in your behavior. Take turns talking and expressing your feelings. Don't interrupt the other person. Listen respectfully to them so that you can truly understand them. Ask God to show you if you are part of the problem. If so, what is your responsibility in solving the issue? Apologize and ask forgiveness if you have been wrong in the situation. Be willing to forgive if necessary. In any conflict between two brothers or sisters in Christ, the goal should always be redemption and reconciliation. God's desire is that there be unity and a bond of love among Christians.

CHAPTER ELEVEN – STUDY QUESTIONS

1. Think of a time in your life when you needed to face a battle with someone. How could you have handled the situation differently?

_____

_____

_____

2. Ask the Lord to show you a situation in your life you need to approach differently. Write below how the Lord answers your question.

_____

_____

_____

3. Write a prayer to God asking Him to give you strength and wisdom to change your approach with this situation.

_____

_____

_____

CHAPTER TWELVE

STEP EIGHT: TAKE UP YOUR POSITION

AN AVID SPORTS FAN WILL tell you that being a team is the key to winning. We all have our favorite sports. One of mine is football. I really enjoy watching teams compete for the crown, at both the college and professional levels of competition. Some teams have one or two great individual players, but few teams can win without all the members playing their own parts. This is clearly seen in the lives of the people of Judah as they faced the battle of their lives. Their lives depended on their strategy for success and their plan gradually unfolded before their eyes. The Bible tells us in verse 17, "You will not need to fight this battle. Stand firm, hold your position, and see the salvation of the Lord on your behalf, O Judah and Jerusalem. Do not be afraid and do not be dismayed. Tomorrow, go out against them, and the Lord will be with you." We have to be careful not to misunderstand when the Scripture says, "You will not need to fight this battle." Some would see written into this a grand capitulation. If I am not going to have to fight, I can just sit here and let the world go by. That is not true in this situation. He immediately follows with, "You will not have to fight that battle, because you are in your position."

Taking up your position in God's economy means you are on the right bus, and sitting in the right seat on the bus, and performing to the best of your ability. In life, and marriage, God has you in a certain position with a specific plan for your life. Psalm 139:16 puts it like this, "Your eyes saw my unformed substance; in your book were written, every one of them, the days that were formed for me, when as yet there was none of them." It is time to take up your God-ordained position.

You probably are asking this question in your mind at this point. *Exactly what is my position?* That answer is different for everyone because God has such a unique plan for every person's life, but there are some generalities that apply in many situations.

For example, if there is a battle with your health, there are certain things that only you can do, like taking your medicine, getting the proper rest, eating healthy foods, and obeying the doctor's orders. There are certain things that only your doctor can do. He can prescribe the right medicine, conduct the right tests, and instruct you to the best of his knowledge. There are certain things that only God can do, like completely healing you from your disease, easing your pain, calming your heart, or knowing when it is time to take you home to heaven. Each person has a position and if every person is in their position, then God can do His work.

When you are facing a battle or difficult position, it is essential to ask God to show you exactly what your position and responsibility is in the situation. When you are taking up your responsibilities and doing everything that only you can do, then God will do His work in a mighty way. There are too many people who consider themselves to be the resident experts when it comes to just about anything and everything in life. All too often such people seek help, but then they talk so much that they never get to benefit from the help they seek. Many who are hurting physically go to the doctor to seek medical treatment, but spend much of the time informing the doctor about the diagnosis they believe suitable for themselves. Perhaps that old time proverb, "you can lead a camel to the water but you cannot make him drink," might have some merit when it comes to this eighth step in God's strategy for success. For sure, no one knows your body better than you do, and it is very important to listen to your own body. Alarms do sound that alert and call for action. But God has surrounded us with so many godly counselors in life. It is best to recognize exactly where you are and what you need to be doing, and then take up your position. Open your heart. And as much as you might be convinced that you need to be the one giving, instead be prepared to sit down, take a deep breath, and be the one receiving. You will be so glad you did.

CHAPTER TWELVE – STUDY QUESTIONS

1.   Think of a current situation in your life in which you are not really taking up your position in the appropriate way. Write briefly what you are not doing and how that is affecting the situation.

_____

_____

_____

2.   Write a prayer asking God to show you what your position is in this situation. Ask Him to speak to your heart and give you a plan.

_____

_____

_____

CHAPTER THIRTEEN

STEP NINE: LET WORSHIP LEAD

THIS SECOND-TO-LAST STEP IS BOUND to capture the attention of the very best of us. God's ways are not our ways, for certain! Jehoshaphat heard God's command through the prophet Jahaziel, and he understood what was going on. He was seeking the face of God, together with all of the people. Interestingly, the latter part of verse 20 says: "Jehoshaphat stood and said, "Hear me, Judah and inhabitants of Jerusalem! Believe in the Lord your God, and you will be established; believe his prophets, and you will succeed." That is wonderful godly counsel, and a wonderful team spirit. Verse 21 continues, "And when he had taken counsel with the people, he appointed those who were to sing to the Lord and praise him in holy attire, as they went before the army, and said, "Give thanks to the Lord, for his steadfast love endures forever." Evidently the choir was mobilized at the *front* of the army!

Some people in the world today would find this a little ironic—if not hilarious! Get this scene clearly pictured in your mind. The army marches out to battle, and Jehoshaphat tells his soldiers to get dressed up, and then just stand there and sing. Maybe you're thinking, *"You've got to be kidding me!"* How much confidence must an army have when its commanding officer sends out a choir to sing ahead of his fighting troops? Can you imagine this happening today? This strategy would seem foolish to many people, but when you let worship lead, you can feel the power and presence of the Lord. When you let worship lead, God sets before us a table from which to eat. Just recently I have witnessed a spiritual surge in our church, in part because worship is leading. It seems that God does inhabit the praise of His people, and that the Spirit of the living God falls in a fresh way on us as we open our hearts in praise and worship to Him. This has been powerfully aided by the call to spend forty days in prayer and fasting before the Lord.

In fact, at the time of the writing of this book, the Lord has laid on my heart to call our church into a time of prayer, fasting, and worship. Our entire church has started forty days of prayer and fasting in some fashion. Some of our people are fasting one day a week. Some are fasting one meal a day. Some are fasting for twenty-one days like Daniel did, and some are fasting for forty days, only drinking water, like Jesus did. There are others who are not able to fast from food because of health issues. So they are fasting from something that is a sacrifice for them personally. The bottom line is this: as a church, we are longing for and seeking the presence of God. We desire a deeper relationship with Him personally and collectively. We are crying out to Him in praise and worship. We are crying out to Him in supplication for our families, our strongholds, and our battles. We are letting worship lead us as we seek Him with all of our hearts. We have already seen miraculous things take place. We have seen people come to receive the Lord after their families have prayed for decades for their salvation. We are seeing fathers and sons reunited after many years of estrangement. We are seeing people gaining a freedom to worship the Lord like we have never experienced in the 175 years of this church. We are crying out to the Lord for revival, and He is bringing it in the hearts and lives of our people. We are sending these services out over the Encouraging Word broadcast and we are crying out to God for the lives of those all over the world who will witness what God is doing. This is not about our church. It is much bigger than that. It is about people all over the United States and all over the world turning to God and worshipping Him with their lives. When this happens, spiritual battles will be won!

And the remarkable thing is our worship leaders are leading all this from the front. Each service of worship begins with worship in praise and song, and this is sustained throughout the entire time of worship. It seems that God is the God of His Word. He does indeed "inhabit the praise of His people"! It feels somewhat like coming home after a long day at the office to find the table all set out and prepared for a scrumptious meal. The setting is as important as the eating and, if one thinks about this long enough, one begins to realize that the setting is a functional part of the eating. There is nothing worse than having to get into an unmade bed at night. On the other hand, is there anything quite as nice as getting into a well-made, aired out, and freshly groomed bed after a long day at the office?

ONE TASTE OF GOD'S GOODNESS WILL
CAUSE YOU TO DESIRE MORE AND MORE.

What would happen if you were to come into God's house with a need so deep for worship that your body ached with a desire to experience the powerful presence of Almighty God? What would happen if you became so enthralled with the precious beauty of God's Word that you became lost in time as you feasted upon the power of His Word? When you let worship lead you, God's Holy Spirit will take control of your heart and life. The Word of God will fight off the enemy and the attacks of the devil. The Word of God is the only offensive part of the Armor of God. At the Word of God, the devil flees. If you let worship lead, you will be successful in the things you do. It worked for Jehoshaphat and it will work for you.

Verse 21 tells us that they kept singing over and over, "Give thanks to the Lord, for His faithful love endures forever." Verse 22 tells us that the moment they began to sing, the Lord set an ambush. Remember, three armies—the Moabites, the Ammonites, and the inhabitants of Mount Seir—were advancing against the people of Judah. These armies did not know each another. The Moabites and the Ammonites turned against the inhabitants of Mount Seir and completely annihilated them. Then, by God's power, those two armies destroyed one another. Not one person was still alive when the battle was over. When Jehoshaphat's singing soldiers arrived at the battlefield, there was nothing left to do but stand there with their mouths gaping, because not one enemy soldier was alive. They, indeed, did not have to fight the battle!

Are you willing to take a taste of God's goodness by worshipping Him with all of your heart? Maybe you have never experienced true worship in your life, and you are not sure if you want to try it or not. When your children are young, they may not want to try vegetables or new foods. Most parents will coax their children to take one taste of everything on their plate. Before you know it, they are eating the whole plate of food. One taste of God's goodness through worship will cause you to desire more and more. Sit before Him daily and drink in His Word, fast, pray, and sing praises to His name. You will be prepared for the attacks of the devil when you grasp His Word in your heart. When you let worship lead, God will fight the battles for you. It is the greatest thing that can happen to you.

CHAPTER THIRTEEN – STUDY QUESTIONS

1. When was the last time you truly worshipped God with all of your heart?

_____

_____

_____

2. Are you willing to set a time to fast and pray and worship God on a regular basis?

_____

_____

_____

3. If your answer to the above question is yes, ask God to show you His plan. How to fast, where to pray, when to pray, where to worship, how to worship Him. Write what he tells you.

_____

_____

_____

STEP TEN: BE AT PEACE

THERE IS NO GREATER FEELING in life than the peace that follows the storm. Peace comes to us as a result of faith and trust in the Lord. The old hymn, "Trust and Obey," is one of my favorites, because it tells us there is no other way to be happy. When we trust God and obey Him, then and only then can we rest in complete peace. Jehoshaphat had done everything he could to obey the Lord. He trusted God completely with his situation, and when God took care of the battle for him, there was a complete peace over the land. Verses 27–30 wrap up the story and give a fantastic example for us to follow when God has completed a wonderful and marvelous conquering of the battles we face in life. Those verses read:

> Then they returned, every man of Judah and Jerusalem, and Jehoshaphat at their head, returning to Jerusalem with joy, for the Lord had made them rejoice over their enemies. They came to Jerusalem with harps and lyres and trumpets, to the house of the Lord. And the fear of God came on all the kingdoms of the countries when they heard that the Lord had fought against the enemies of Israel. So the realm of Jehoshaphat was quiet, for his God gave him rest all around.

When you have done everything God has called you to do, be at peace with your situation. Being at peace means that you trust God completely. Philippians 4:6–7 tells us, "Do not be anxious about anything, but in everything by prayer and supplication with thanksgiving let your requests be made known to God. And the peace of God, which passes all understanding, will guard your hearts and your minds in Christ Jesus."

DO NOT BE ANXIOUS ABOUT ANYTHING.

Do you have a hard time trusting God with your battles? I do at times. It is easy to try and take things into our own hands and try to work out our problems. It can be hard to wait on God and completely trust Him. I wonder how the battle would have turned out if Jehoshaphat had gone ahead of God? Many times I've made a mess of situations in my life because I ran ahead of God and tried to fight the battle on my own! If you truly want peace in your life and want to overcome your battles, give it over to God, obey Him completely, and trust Him to work out things the way He sees fit. Sometimes God doesn't do it the way we would want or expect, but He always does it according to His will. And His will for our lives is always best! No matter what we have to walk through, He will be there to walk beside us, fight for us, and give us peace that passes all understanding when we trust Him completely.

CHAPTER FOURTEEN – STUDY QUESTIONS

1. Look in the front of this book at the table of contents and list the ten steps God gave to Jehoshaphat to win the battle. You will find the steps as the titles of Chapters 5–14.

_____

_____

_____

_____

_____

_____

_____

_____

_____

_____

2. Ask God to show you how to utilize these steps in your daily life to conquer a specific battle you are facing. Write what He tells you below.

_____

_____

_____

CHAPTER FIFTEEN

CONCLUSION: CELEBRATE THE VICTORY

THE STORY OF THE HEALING of the ten lepers is one that always leaves a sad note in my heart. It makes me sad to think that the Lord Jesus did what He alone could do—He healed them all—and yet only one of them returned to say thank you. All too often this is a picture of us. Hurricanes blow through our neighborhoods, the Twin Towers are savagely attacked, people cry out to God and are healed, finances run out but the Lord provides, and the list goes on. But how soon we forget! And how seldom we stop to give thanks to God! Not so with Jehoshaphat and his people. They were at peace, and so they celebrated with song and thanksgiving to the Lord.

When you have done everything you can do, and you completely trust in the Lord, He will fight the battles for you. When the battles are won, take time to celebrate what God has done in your life. Like Jehoshaphat, maybe the battle didn't end the way you thought it would, but know that God is working and He knows what is best for you. His ways are not our ways, so sometimes we would like for life to take a different direction. Sometimes God works out the situation as we hoped and He even gives us more than we ever dreamed possible! But know this: God will walk with you through the trials and battles of life. He will prove His faithfulness to you every time. When you trust in God with all your heart, you will have a successful life in His eyes.

GOD WILL WALK WITH YOU THROUGH THE TRIALS AND BATTLES OF LIFE.

At this point, I pray that God has put the big picture of success into your mind and heart. Strive for the success that will give you joy and peace. Work toward acquiring the kind of success that will enable you to look back with no regret and no sorrow. When you face the Lord Jesus, He will say, "Welcome home; well done, good and faithful servant!"

What beachhead do you need to set up today? Are you facing a battle that you know you cannot fight on your own? What principles do you need to adopt into your life to lead you in the right direction? What strategy do you need to follow? Is God calling you to stand up and be the husband and father you need to be for your family? Is He calling you to set up a beachhead in your place of business or community to conquer the battles? Is He calling you to fast and pray, and worship Him with all of your heart? Is He calling you to seek His presence and find your identity in Him? Listen to Him and obey whatever he tells you to do.

I pray that God will burn the core values of integrity, accountability, purity, and humility into your heart and give you a strategy to take your life back. I pray that He will give you a strategy to become successful in His eyes. I pray that you will seek God's presence and that you will rest in His peace for your life. When you and I come into His presence and we cry out to Him, "Take my life. Lead me, Lord. I am Yours, and Yours alone," be assured that He will hear you. He loves you, and He has a hope and a bright future planned for you. God is on His throne, and His desire for you and for me is to live a full and a meaningful life in Christ.

When you seek the presence of God with all of your heart, He will speak to you. Listen to Him and do whatever He says. You will find that your battles are conquered, and you will have a successful life filled with peace that passes all understanding, because He is walking beside you every step of the way. Celebrate that victory today as you rest in His peace.

CHAPTER FIFTEEN – STUDY QUESTIONS

1. Write a prayer to God expressing what you have learned in this book. Tell Him what you think He is calling you to do at this point in your life. Share your prayer to God with a Christian friend you trust. You may share it with someone at The Encouraging Word by calling the number in the back of the book. We would love to pray for you!

_____

_____

_____

NOTES

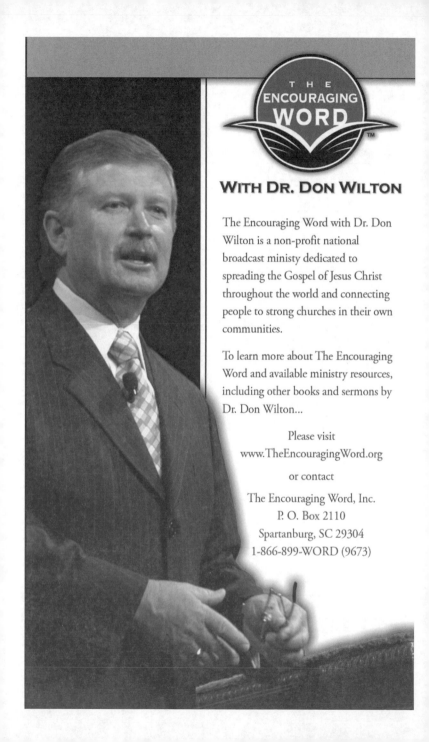

THE ENCOURAGING WORD

WITH DR. DON WILTON

The Encouraging Word with Dr. Don Wilton is a non-profit national broadcast ministy dedicated to spreading the Gospel of Jesus Christ throughout the world and connecting people to strong churches in their own communities.

To learn more about The Encouraging Word and available ministry resources, including other books and sermons by Dr. Don Wilton...

Please visit
www.TheEncouragingWord.org

or contact

The Encouraging Word, Inc.
P. O. Box 2110
Spartanburg, SC 29304
1-866-899-WORD (9673)

For more information about
Don Wilton
&
Undefeated
God's Strategy for Successful Living
please visit:

www.TheEncouragingWord.org

For more information about
AMBASSADOR INTERNATIONAL
please visit:

www.ambassador-international.com
@AmbassadorIntl
www.facebook.com/AmbassadorIntl